The Little Book of
Appreciation

Also by Francis Briers:

A little book on finding your Way:
Zen and the Art of Doing stuff

Warrior Philosophy in Game of Thrones

And soon to be released...

My Tao Te Ching: A Fools Guide to Effing
the Ineffable

The Wisdom Economy

The Little Book of Appreciation

By

Francis Briers

Warriors of Love Publishing

Acknowledgements

I have been assisted, supported, taught, mentored, and loved by many people over the years in my personal development, writing, and living. My mum, Lyn and my dad, Fred have always been so supportive, and my wife Miche and son Samson who are continuing that tradition have to be top of this list.

I owe a great deal to my fellow facilitators and learning junkies: Lance Giroux from whom I learned so much about facilitation; Mette Jacobsgaard and Jane Magruder Watkins from whom I first learned about Appreciative Inquiry; Jamie Morgan, soul-brother and fellow mischief-maker; Claire Breeze and Sue Cheshire, corporate fairy-godmothers; Leanne Lowish and the team at Axialent with whom I continue to explore and deepen appreciation in practice; Andy Bradley, Kirsty Murray and the team at Frameworks4Change from whom I have learned and with whom I have shared so much. Judy Piatkus for huge generosity and wisdom.

Thank you all for your care and support.

Contents

Introduction

I think we live in an appreciation-starved world. Maybe there are places where this isn't the case but for the most part in the places I have visited, worked in, or I have worked with people from; the norm seems to be to point out problems and if it's good then ignore it and hope it keeps happening. Both my instincts and several bodies of research[*] seem to suggest that, not only is this not a very caring, humane way to relate to each other and our world, it is also not a very effective one. In working with many people from all over the world I have often seen them struggle with appreciating each other at first. I think there are various reasons for this but one of them seems to be that we don't

---

[*] See the section towards the end of the book if you want to read about this

have the language for it. We are out of the habit of appreciation and have lost the necessary tools. So I made this book to help with that.

What I have seen is that once people get into the habit of appreciating themselves and each other, this small, simple act seems to breathe new life into the person giving the appreciation, the one receiving it, and into their relationship. Whether you are someone's colleague, boss, husband, wife, friend, sister, brother, mother, father, or child, I can assure you that receiving a little appreciation regularly can make a huge difference to people's lives and well-being. I have seen it time and again. It may be a little uncomfortable at first, it may feel a little strange, but once you get used to it, it feels wonderful. Very little worth doing is achieved without some discomfort, especially if it means making a change.

So, if you want to be part of this gentle revolution, here's the basics:

Begin with the sentence root -

"What I appreciate about you is your..."

Then find the word that most precisely describes what you find wonderful about that person in this moment and finish your sentence with that word. The more specific you can be, the more likely you will speak with authenticity and the more likely the person you are appreciating will be able to receive what you are saying and 'let it land.' There's an 'advanced class' at the end of the book you can check out but even one word, carefully chosen can have a huge impact when offered with real care. I know for myself that when someone has clearly considered what they are going to say and chooses a word that, even in my possible embarrassment or discomfort, I can recognise as resonating with a quality they have seen in me, it lands. It lands in me and I feel seen for the gifts I bring to the world both deliberately and just because of who I am. I have stood with groups sharing literally one-word appreciations without even the beginning of the sentence and seen people light up, warmed and affirmed by the positive feedback in their friends' and colleague's appreciation.

There is skill in receiving appreciation too, and this comes with practice as well. The basics of that is:

1. Really listen to and hear what the person has to say

2. Breathe and let it land

That's it!

So, with love and respect, I dare you, I double dare you to go out there and appreciate the people in your life; then watch the way that we can all contribute to making the world a better place, one word at a time.

A little note on the format: You'll see on each page there is the sentence root at the top of the page to remind you, then one word featured on that page. With the word is a brief description of how someone who really embodies that word might be, and a quote to further give you a feel. If these are helpful then great! However, don't get caught up in my descriptions or chosen quotes. If the word resonates and you have your own sense of it's meaning, go with that. The descriptions and quotes are there to inspire you, not restrict your own sense of meaning.

101
Words
of
Appreciation

The Little Book of Appreciation
"What I appreciate about you is your..."

Strength

Some people just exhibit an amazing kind of strength. Sometimes they are those physically strong people who embody something that means we feel that nothing can shake them Sometimes it is nothing to do with physicality but to do with the fact they have faced profound challenges in their life and are still walking tall.

Strength does not come from winning. Your struggles develop your strengths. When you go through hardships and decide not to surrender, that is strength.

- Arnold Schwarzenegger

Gracefulness

Some people bring a sense of gentleness, warmth and beauty to what they do, and perhaps a kind of effortlessness which is a joy to be around and can inspire us to find more flow in what we do.

There's a trick to the Graceful Exit. It begins with the vision to recognize when a job, a life stage, a relationship is over - and to let go. It means leaving what's over without denying its value.

- Ellen Goodman

Beauty

This can be associated with physical beauty, but it's also to do with someone's quality of presence and what they offer. Some people, just by their presence, wherever they go, make the environment more beautiful either by the things they create or the attention they offer people.

People are like stained - glass windows. They sparkle and shine when the sun is out, but when the darkness sets in, their true beauty is revealed only if there is a light from within.

- Elisabeth Kubler-Ross

Solidity

There are those people in our lives that are our 'rocks' who we know we can always depend on. Sometimes we feel this because we know them well but some people just have this about them: you can tell they can be relied upon.

The strongest thing that any human being has going is their own integrity and their own heart. As soon as you start veering away from that, the solidity that you need in order to be able to stand up for what you believe in and deliver what's really inside, it's just not going to be there.

- *Herbie Hancock*

Faith

This quality doesn't need to be religious. Some people just have that aura of trust in the world, the process, their fellow human beings which helps the rest of us feel a little less fearful in the face of life's challenges.

Faith is taking the first step even when you don't see the whole staircase.

- Martin Luther King, Jr.

Expertise

Working alongside someone who is deeply expert at what they do can be such a gift. Some people seem to enjoy gathering knowledge and expertise and those of us who are fortunate enough to work with them benefit from the learning and reassurance we can derive from their presence.

You must continue to gain expertise, but avoid thinking like an expert.

- Denis Waitley

Wisdom

Depth of insight and being at ease with life's mysteries; to be able to hold and handle them without needing to 'solve' or 'fix' them.

Wisdom doesn't consist of knowing specific facts or possessing knowledge of a field. It consists of knowing how to treat knowledge: being confident but not too confident; adventurous but grounded. It is a willingness to confront counter-evidence and to have a feel for the vast spaces beyond what's known.

- David Brooks

Presence

This can have two interpretations. One is that someone is really present, in the moment, here and now, and able to be with whatever emerges. The other is that you may not be able to pin down why, but you appreciate someone's presence – just the way they turn up with you is reassuring and supportive.

I teach people that no matter what the situation is, no matter how chaotic, no matter how much drama is around you, you can heal by your presence if you just stay within your centre.

- Deepak Chopra

Mindfulness

With a quiet mind this person's every action is considered and filled with care.

Mindfulness is about love and loving life. When you cultivate this love, it gives you clarity and compassion for life, and your actions happen in accordance with that.

- Jon Kabat-Zinn

Thoughtfulness

You can tell that this person thinks carefully about those around them, and the impact they have on the world. They often notice the little things that others miss.

Never doubt that a small group of thoughtful, committed citizens can change the world; indeed, it's the only thing that ever has.

- Margaret Mead

Care

There is a deep well of caring that just flows out of some people. They bring loving attention to those around them and constantly seek to look after everyone they meet.

Nobody cares how much you know, until they know how much you care.

- Theodore Roosevelt

Courage

Bravery in the face of challenge. People can be physically courageous, but people can be brave with their emotions too: in their honesty, in their relationships, and in how they challenge their beliefs or ways of thinking.

"Many people today believe that cynicism requires courage. Actually, cynicism is the height of cowardice. It is innocence and open-heartedness that requires the true courage - however often we are hurt as a result of it."

- Erica Jong

Playfulness

Someone who brings a gentle sense of fun and play into what they do making it more joyful for everyone.

There often seems to be a playfulness to wise people, as if either their equanimity has as its source this playfulness or the playfulness flows from the equanimity; and they can persuade other people who are in a state of agitation to calm down and manage a smile.

- Edward Hoagland

Humour

Some people are just funny! They help us laugh at life and ourselves in a way that brightens the day.

There's no life without humour. It can make the wonderful moments of life truly glorious, and it can make tragic moments bearable.

- Rufus Wainwright

Generosity

Whether it is clearly considered and thought through, or just seems to be the way someone is; some people are unusually generous. They give of themselves, their time, their energy, their food, their resources of all kinds. Whatever it is that they give, giving seems to be in their nature.

Many men have been capable of doing a wise thing, more a cunning thing, but very few a generous thing.

- Alexander Pope

Brightness

Like a cool breeze through a room, some people have a clarity, a kind of alertness and presence which means they brighten the room when they walk in.

The true optimist not only expects the best to happen, but goes to work to make the best happen. The true optimist not only looks upon the bright side, but trains every force that is in him to produce more and more brightness in his life...

- Christian D. Larson

Intelligence

Some people are not only very intelligent but also wield that intelligence skilfully, in a way that helps others.

The test of a first-rate intelligence is the ability to hold two opposed ideas in the mind at the same time, and still retain the ability to function.

- F. Scott Fitzgerald

Knowledge

It can be so supportive to have someone around who really knows what they are talking about! Knowledge, skilfully shared, can be such a gift.

A people without the knowledge of their past history, origin and culture is like a tree without roots.

- Marcus Garvey

Compassion

To see not only when someone needs help but what kind of help will best serve them, and the big-heartedness to be able to offer it. To not just 'make it OK' but to help people flourish and grow into the best versions of themselves.

Compassion is not a relationship between the healer and the wounded. It's a relationship between equals. Only when we know our own darkness well can we be present with the darkness of others. Compassion becomes real when we recognize our shared humanity.

- Pema Chodron

Fierceness

The passion and grit and commitment to really go after what you want, to create what you care about and protect it when it's threatened. Fierceness born of love and care and dedication.

We can learn the art of fierce compassion - redefining strength, deconstructing isolation & renewing a sense of community, practicing letting go of rigid us-vs.-them thinking - while cultivating power and clarity in response to difficult situations.

- Sharon Salzberg

Passion

People driven by their own passion evoke that passion in all the rest of us. Not necessarily about the same thing, but by allowing themselves space, and having the courage to pursue their passions they show us all it's possible and set us thinking about what we care about that much.

Great dancers are not great because of their technique, they are great because of their passion.

- Martha Graham

Nurture

Nurturing means caring for, tending to, encouraging, helping to grow, and in all of that creating a safe space for others and what they need.

We've got this gift of love, but love is like a precious plant. You can't just accept it and leave it in the cupboard or just think it's going to get on by itself. You've got to keep watering it. You've got to really look after it and nurture it.

- John Lennon

Dedication

Sometimes this looks like a real deep commitment to a particular cause or perspective - to bringing that to every moment with consistency and power. Sometimes it is a more general sense of keeping turning up every day with a stalwart consistency that we know means this person can be depended on: they're dedicated.

Confidence doesn't come out of nowhere. It's a result of something... hours and days and weeks and years of constant work and dedication.

- Roger Staubach

Commitment

Some people commit to what they do with their whole being and that can be a wonderful and supportive thing for those around them. Whether it's something they embody all the time or how they turn up when doing something specific, it can be a great quality to witness.

The quality of a person's life is in direct proportion to their commitment to excellence, regardless of their chosen field of endeavour.

- Vince Lombardi

Flamboyance

This 'larger-than-life' quality can help us all feel a little freer, more expressive, and generous-spirited. When one person allows themselves to live a big life that can inspire the rest of us.

To change one's life:
1. Start immediately.
2. Do it flamboyantly.
3. No exceptions.

- William James

Diligence

Hard-working, thorough, interested in the details, just keeping going, head down and make it happen!

Diligence is the mother of good fortune.

- Benjamin Disraeli

Elegance

A grace and beauty about how this person conducts themselves which elevates the quality of what they do. This can be obvious to spot when it is physical elegance but sometimes people can be elegant thinkers, or come up with elegant solutions to problems too.

The only real elegance is in the mind; if you've got that, the rest really comes from it.

- *Diana Vreeland*

Hospitality

Someone who invites people into their space and offers a warm welcome to those they meet. There is a firm but gentle caring for others, and an active creation of warm spaces for others. We feel at home in their presence.

The word 'hospitality' in the New Testament comes from two Greek words. The first word means 'love' and the second word means 'strangers.' It's a word that means love of strangers.

- Nancy Leigh DeMoss

Insight

A capacity to see into the heart of things, to perceive things others don't, and come to an understanding of life which is rare and when shared helps others to find new perspectives.

A moment's insight is sometimes worth a life's experience.

- Oliver Wendell Holmes, Jr.

Creativity

An artist or someone who approaches life and it's challenges in such a way that they see possibilities, novelty, and options where others see a single path.

One very important aspect of motivation is the willingness to stop and to look at things that no one else has bothered to look at. This simple process of focusing on things that are normally taken for granted is a powerful source of creativity.

- Edward de Bono

Daring

Someone adventurous who is willing to take risks and go out on a limb. Their marvellous journey can inspire all of us to stretch a little more and find our own.

Life is either a daring adventure or nothing.

- Helen Keller

Inclusiveness

Some people gather and include people by their nature, or by their thoughtfulness. Everyone feels welcomed and included by them.

We are less when we don't include everyone

- Stuart Milk

Fairness

Whether being gentle or tough this person treats everyone equally with an even hand. You never feel like they are unjustly biased.

Live so that when your children think of fairness and integrity, they think of you.

— H. Jackson Brown Jr.

Warmth

There is a sense of welcome and generosity of spirit about this person which means that when you meet them the world feels a little warmer.

One looks back with appreciation to the brilliant teachers, but with gratitude to those who touched our human feelings. The curriculum is so much necessary raw material, but warmth is the vital element for the growing plant and for the soul of the child.

- Carl Jung

Ingenuity

Always finding new and inventive solutions, showing a dexterity of mind.

Never tell people how to do things. Tell them what to do and they will surprise you with their ingenuity.

- George S. Patton

Honesty

One of those people who always tells the truth. At times it may not be easy to hear but you can trust that whatever they say, they believe to be true.

No legacy is so rich as honesty.

- William Shakespeare

Openness

Like an open door or an open book this person seems … open! Open to life, to people, to experiences and opportunity.

The purpose of education is to replace an empty mind with an open one.

- Malcolm Forbes

Directness

This person is a straight-talker. They may be challenging at times but it is well intended and you can depend on them to get straight to the point.

Confidence is directness and courage in meeting the facts of life.

- John Dewey

Intensity

Someone who dives deep by their nature engaging with life fiercely and meeting challenges with power and grit.

Always work hard. Intensity clarifies. It creates not only momentum, but also the pressure you need to feel either friction, or fulfilment.

- Marcus Buckingham

Calmness

We all wobble in life at time but people with this quality seem to wobble less, keeping calm even amongst difficulty and their calm helps the rest of us to keep our feet a little better too. A cool head even in a storm.

The more tranquil a man becomes, the greater is his success, his influence, his power for good. Calmness of mind is one of the beautiful jewels of wisdom.

- James Allen

Peacefulness

Someone who seems at peace in themselves and by their presence helps others to feel more peaceful too.

Nobody can bring you peace but yourself.

- Ralph Waldo Emerson

Innocence

Some people seem to manage to preserve in themselves an unspoiled quality lacking cynicism, un-jaded by life.

There is an innocence in admiration; it is found in those to whom it has never yet occurred that they, too, might be admired someday.

- Friedrich Nietzsche

Simplicity

Some people embody and express a kind of minimalism and clarity which makes them uncomplicated. No frills, always just what's needed.

Simplicity   is   the   ultimate sophistication.

- Leonardo da Vinci

Helpfulness

Some people always seem to help. Maybe it's just how they are, or perhaps it is part of how they mindfully meet the world, but either way when someone needs help it's often them there giving a hand.

No matter how you try to make the world a better place, the first step always starts with helping each other.

- Magith Noohukhan

Amiability

Easy to get on with. Buoyant in a gentle way.   Making light, easy connections everywhere they go.

Amiable people ... radiate so much of mental sunshine that they are reflected in all appreciative hearts.

- Madame Dorothe Deluzy

Dependability

Someone you can count on who keeps turning up, keeps doing what's needed, day after day. You know they'll always be there.

Dependability is that quality of sureness which makes folks know that the task assigned will be accomplished, that the promise made will be kept, a golden quality.

- Clarissa A. Beesley

Curiosity

One of those people who's interested in everything almost beyond reason! No matter how much they may know or learn they keep an open mind, always enquiring, seeking to understand.

Curiosity is the leading edge of love.

- John Young

Innovation

Someone who is always looking for the latest, most creative and most useful ways to get things done. A solution is not good enough, they want the best solution and they've never met a situation that couldn't be improved!

Dreamers are mocked as impractical. The truth is they are the most practical, as their innovations lead to progress and a better way of life for all of us.

- Robin S. Sharma

Smile

Some people always have a smile on their face and others have one that appears like the sun from behind a cloud and lights the room. Whatever kind it is, some people's smiles brighten our days and that is a beautiful thing.

Too often we underestimate the power of a touch, a smile, a kind word, a listening ear, an honest compliment, or the smallest act of caring, all of which have the potential to turn a life around.

- Leo Buscaglia

Open-heartedness

This person offers an unconditional, non-judgemental welcome to whoever they meet. They carry a warm and caring space everywhere they go.

Deep listening is miraculous for both listener and speaker. When someone receives us with open-hearted, non-judging, intensely interested listening, our spirits expand.

- Sue Patton Thoele

Gentleness

Treading lightly in the world, bringing a warm and soft touch to every interaction. A tender care in every moment.

Nothing is so strong as gentleness, nothing so gentle as real strength.

- Saint Francis de Sales

Clarity

A quality of seeing clearly and being able to share that clear vision with others. Someone with this quality can help us all have a cleaner, clearer perspective on things. The world just seems less muddy with them in it!

I thought the dulling of perception was an inevitable consequence of age - just as a lens of the eye is bound gradually to dim. I didn't understand that clarity is in the mind.

- Keith Johnstone

Kindness

Some people either due to their nature or the way they mindfully approach the world bring an attitude of kindness to everyone they meet and to the situations they face. There is a gentle care in the way they approach the world.

Kindness is the language which the deaf can hear and the blind can see.

- Mark Twain

Respect

Many of us have a basic level of respect for the people we meet, work and live with, but some people seem to embody respect in such a way that they bring a heightened dignity to their conversations, and people grow and naturally offer respect in return.

"Love" is the radical respect of the other as a legitimate other.

- Humberto Maturana

Sweetness

One of those people who by their sweet nature bring a smile to your face whenever you see them. Sometimes they're quiet people, easy to miss, but once noticed they are a delight to be around and gently lift other's spirits.

Gratitude is the sweetest thing in a seeker's life- in all human life. If there is gratitude in your heart, then there will be tremendous sweetness in your eyes.

- *Sri Chinmoy*

Tenderness

A capacity to meet the wounded place in others with a kind of nurture and sensitivity which allows people to stay with their pain but feel held and safe.

When we honestly ask ourselves which person in our lives means the most to us, we often find that it is those who, instead of giving advice, solutions, or cures, have chosen rather to share our pain and touch our wounds with a warm and tender hand.

- Henri Nouwen

Spirit

Some people are just filled with spirit! Their bright eyes and general zest for life is infectious and regardless of their age there is a vigour about them that encourages us all to find the spring in our step.

Never underestimate the power of dreams and the influence of the human spirit. We are all the same in this notion: The potential for greatness lives within each of us.

- Wilma Rudolph

Spark

One of those people that lights fires in others through their passion. There is a fire which burns brightly in them which skips like a spark struck from a flint and steel to land in us and reveal the fire in us too.

At times our own light goes out and is rekindled by a spark from another person. Each of us has cause to think with deep gratitude of those who have lighted the flame within us.

- Albert Schweitzer

Lightness

Some people have a lightness about them which lifts a situation. They are like a breath of fresh air, shifting things, and lifting the atmosphere without stirring up the situation or creating a drama.

I talk about very serious human affairs but with a lightness of heart.

- Robert Fulghum

Flow

A quality of fluidity and grace which makes situations easier to move through, transitions easier to manage, and creates a sense of continuity from one action to another. We can dance through the day instead of plodding.

May what I do flow from me like a river, no forcing and no holding back, the way it is with children.

- Rainer Maria Rilke

Flexibility

One of those people who is able to turn their hand to whatever needs doing. They may not always know how to do it but they are happy to ask and be guided and the flexibility is about their attitude to life. If we can't do it one way let's find another.

Flexibility means being able to make problems into teachers.

- Dadi Janki

Serenity

Serenity combines peacefulness with a kind of beauty. There is a peaceful quietness in this person's presence that we don't want to break. There is a slow gracefulness they radiate which helps us all calm down.

Boredom is the feeling that everything is a waste of time; serenity, that nothing is.

- Thomas Szasz

Steadiness

This person is consistent in a way that you know you can rely on. They keep moving and have a solid kind of momentum that means you know they will get there. They don't wobble or falter, they just keep taking the next step no matter what.

Be steady and well-ordered in your life so that you can be fierce and original in your work.

- *Gustave Flaubert*

Feistiness

One of those people who stands up for what they believe in, who'll give you a run for your money. Enjoyably fierce, we love them even when they challenge us.

It's about being alive and feisty and not sitting down and shutting up. Even if people would like you to.

- Pink

Constancy

They are always there when you need them, they turn up again and again, they are like a star you can navigate by: a constant in the changing world.

I have always argued that change becomes stressful and overwhelming only when you've lost any sense of the constancy of your life. You need firm ground to stand on. From there, you can deal with that change.

- Richard Nelson Bolles

Preciseness

One of those people who gets things right every time, not because they want to be clever but just because they deeply value accuracy. You can trust them because they know where, and what, and when, and how. They've designed it down to the last millimetre.

Concision in style, precision in thought, decision in life.

- Victor Hugo

Freeness

Some people just seem to embody freedom. They are the classic 'free spirit' not tied to anything. They help the rest of us break our shackles once in a while and may even inspire us to let go of what we have to explore new possibilities in a larger sense.

For to be free is not merely to cast off one's chains, but to live in a way that respects and enhances the freedom of others.

- Nelson Mandela

Depth

One of life's deep divers. No matter where you go or what you are experiencing, this person can go with you. They contemplate the big questions and delve in dark places. This gives them insight, compassion for the human condition, and a capacity to make sense of the world and share that wisdom.

It is not length of life, but depth of life.

- Ralph Waldo Emerson

Perspective

This person can keep hold of the big picture even in challenging times. They are often the voice of reason when others are struggling not to jump into reactivity or even panic. They are able to take a step back and be less attached to the outcome which enables reflectiveness and clarity.

You must look within for value, but must look beyond for perspective.

- Denis Waitley

Objectivity

An ability to be emotionally unattached which means they can hold all sides equally and separate out opinion from fact.

Dispassionate objectivity is itself a passion, for the real and for the truth.

- Abraham Maslow

Gravitas

Someone you naturally take seriously. When they speak people listen and their opinions are trusted. Sometimes this is because of deep expertise but sometimes it is just a quality someone has: what they say carries weight.

I gravitate towards gravitas

- Morgan Freeman

Humility

This person never overestimates their own knowledge and welcomes other people's perspectives. They have a profound sense of how much lies beyond the realm of their experience.

We learned about gratitude and humility - that so many people had a hand in our success, from the teachers who inspired us to the janitors who kept our school clean... and we were taught to value everyone's contribution and treat everyone with respect.

- Michelle Obama

Wildness

These people habitually break free of convention and seem to live with the power and passion of a force of nature. Maybe they remind you of wide-open spaces or the unbounded creative energy of deep woodland – life springing up everywhere. Sometimes they challenge us but they also help us to rediscover our own wild spirit too.

When I die, I want people to play my music, go wild and freak out and do anything they want to do.

- Jimi Hendrix

Sparkle

Some people are just sparkly! With a twinkle in their eye, a sweetness to their nature, and a smile that speaks of playful mischief, these people put a bit of magic in a dull day.

We need less posturing and more genuine charisma. It's about a sparkle in people money can't buy

- Marianne Williamson

Imagination

This person sees possibility and story in everything and can bring whole other worlds to life.

Imagination is not only the uniquely human capacity to envision that which is not, and, therefore, the foundation of all invention and innovation. In its arguably most transformative and revelatory capacity, it is the power that enables us to empathize with humans whose experiences we have never shared.

- J.K. Rowling

Selflessness

Always giving. Giving generously with no thought for their own gain, this person is always looking out for others.

Only those who have learned the power of sincere and selfless contribution experience life's deepest joy: true fulfilment.

- Tony Robbins

Vivaciousness

This person is full of life and spirit and shares this generously with everyone. They light up the room when they walk in and can be the life and soul of any event.

Wake up and greet each and every day with a vivacious spirit and positive attitude!

- *Melanie M. Koulouris*

Joyfulness

Some people are not only joyful themselves but carry that joy near the surface which enables the rest of us to benefit from it. They bring joy with them and leave a place better than when they found it.

Joy in looking and comprehending is nature's most beautiful gift.

- Albert Einstein

Guts

No matter the scale of the challenge you can depend on this person to dig deep and dive in. Theirs is not a showy kind of bravery; there is a kind of dogged determination that you've got to admire.

Gold medals aren't really made of gold. They're made of sweat, determination, and a hard-to-find alloy called guts.

- Dan Gable

Determination

They just keep going. They are resolute and will steadily keep going to achieve their goals. If they jump on board to help you then they can lend you that solid and persistent momentum they carry and it helps you keep going too.

We all have dreams. But in order to make dreams come into reality, it takes an awful lot of determination, dedication, self-discipline, and effort.

- Jesse Owens

Focus

A capacity to bring full attention in each moment, each task, and a clarity about what you are working on and creating in what you do.

The successful warrior is the average man, with laser-like focus.

- Bruce Lee

Integrity

You can depend on this person to do what they say they will, but more than that, they hold themselves to a very strong standard of what is right and honest. They seek to embody the spirit of a commitment, not just the letter of the law.

Real integrity is doing the right thing, knowing that nobody's going to know whether you did it or not.

- Oprah Winfrey

Love

Some people consistently offer a lot of love to the world, and not just to those they are closest to but to everyone they meet. These people bring an openness and warmth to their interactions as a matter of habit.

Love is the ability and willingness to allow those that you care for to be what they choose for themselves without any insistence that they satisfy you.

- Wayne Dyer

Mentoring

A wisdom and richness of experience which is generously shared by helping others to learn and grow.

The delicate balance of mentoring someone is not creating them in your own image, but giving them the opportunity to create themselves.

- Steven Spielberg

Leadership

Someone who stands as an example in what they do and influences others to bring their best game. Sometimes very visible, sometimes subtly supportive, great leaders enable others to shine and groups to achieve great things.

I start with the premise that the function of leadership is to produce more leaders, not more followers.

- Ralph Nader

Decisiveness

Whether intuitive or swift to assess a situation (or a bit of both) this person is able to come to conclusions fast and then act on their choices. They combine insight and the courage of their convictions.

Decisiveness is a characteristic of high-performing men and women. Almost any decision is better than no decision at all.

- Brian Tracy

Vision

This person can find clarity in the chaos of life and imagine what's possible. They can craft a vision of the future and share it in such a way that we are empowered to work towards a better world - whether that's the small world of our immediate environment & relationships or the wider world we all share.

Vision is the art of seeing what is invisible to others.

- Jonathan Swift

Subtlety

The capacity to act with care and attention to the degree that those actions are no less effective but create much less disturbance than you'd expect. It's like these people can cross the river without disturbing the flow.

The world communicates subtly. Most people don't hear or see the signs because they're so wrapped up in their day-to-day lives."

- Doug Cooper

Eloquence

Someone with this quality is able to communicate their thinking in an elegant and fluid way. They speak skilfully without necessarily needing to talk a lot, each word well-chosen but effortless.

Talking and eloquence are not the same: to speak and to speak well are two things. A fool may talk, but a wise man speaks.

- Heinrich Heine

Expressiveness

Someone who naturally shares who they are with the world in a genuine and generous way: warm, animated, and playful.

I want freedom for the full expression of my personality.

- *Mahatma Gandhi*

Stability

This person has a steadiness and quality of balance. You know where you stand with them and can rely on their constancy even in tough times.

Valour is stability, not of legs and arms, but of courage and the soul.

- Michel de Montaigne

Adventurousness

One of those people who just embraces every opportunity to explore the world and dive into life. Someone who embodies this quality likes to find the edges, to find the possibilities, to try things out and see where it takes them.

I like someone who embraces life; who wants to be on a long journey but has no particular plan or destination in mind. An adventurous man, open to the concept of living life in the moment.

- *Jill Hennessy*

Efficiency

The capacity to find the quickest route, the swiftest way, the most pared-down approach to solving any problem. It can be such a gift to have someone like this on your team as they help us all get more done and make space for what matters most.

The highest and best form of efficiency is the spontaneous cooperation of a free people.

- Woodrow Wilson

Intuition

Some people are better at listening to their intuitive nudges than others. They are guided by their feelings and notice things others miss which can help us all to discover new ways of seeing life.

Your time is limited, so don't waste it living someone else's life. Don't be trapped by dogma - which is living with the results of other people's thinking. Don't let the noise of others' opinions drown out your own inner voice. And most important, have the courage to follow your heart and intuition.

- Steve Jobs

Awesomeness!

Sometimes someone does something so amazing that they are just awesome! At times appreciation can be as playful as it is heartfelt. Noticing the moments of awesomeness we all have can be a lovely, fun way to say "thank you for being your wonderful self!"

Beliefs have the power to create and the power to destroy. Human beings have the awesome ability to take any experience of their lives and create a meaning that dis-empowers them or one that can literally save their lives.

- Tony Robbins

Skill

Some people achieve a level of dexterity and finesse in something they do that is wonderful to watch, and if it involves doing something that affects us then it can be a real gift to have them help us.

When love and skill work together, expect a masterpiece.

- John Ruskin

Style

That quality where, when this person is in the room, or does something you think to yourself "Now that's a class act!"

Fashion fades, only style remains the same.

- Coco Chanel

Vulnerability

This can be an underrated quality but the capacity and willingness to allow others to see who you really are even when it might be painful can be such a gift. It gives permission for us all to be more human. It creates intimacy.

When we were children, we used to think that when we were grown-up we would no longer be vulnerable. But to grow up is to accept vulnerability... To be alive is to be vulnerable.

- Madeleine L'Engle

Showmanship

Maybe they have a particular skill, or maybe it's just when speaking to people or interacting socially, but whatever they do, this person does it with flair and an ability to play to an audience. They can make the world seem brighter for a while and it's a great joy to be around this natural entertainer.

The secret of showmanship consists not of what you really do, but what the mystery-loving public thinks you do.

- Harry Houdini

Challenge

This could involve challenging someone who's out of line or doing sub-standard work, or encouraging someone to stretch themselves because they have more potential than they are showing. Either way, to challenge someone is tough. To do it well, so that you are heard but don't offend, takes real skill.

Sometimes those who challenge you most, teach you best.

- Anonymous

Charisma

That hard-to-define mix of warmth, openness, graciousness, and sheer energy which makes someone easy to like and a natural influencer of others.

Charm is an intangible. Chutzpah, charm, charisma, that kind of thing, you can't buy it. You either have it or you don't.

- Colm Feore

When both giving and receiving appreciations:

Remember to breathe!

Appendices

How
To Use
This If You
Are...

...In a relationship

Life can be tough, and even when it's not tough it is frequently busy. So, it is no wonder that at times we struggle or even fail to appreciate our loved ones as much as we would wish to in our best moments. As my friend Clare Myatt says: "practice makes permanent," so why not make a practice of appreciating your partner, husband, wife, child, or any and all of your loved ones. When it's left to chance, appreciation can be patchy; so why not set aside a few minutes every day, maybe at the end of your day together to offer each other appreciations? How much more loved, seen, and valued might you and your loved ones feel if you were appreciated every day without fail?

See the advanced class for more practice ideas

...A Manager

As a manager I found it very easy to get caught up in meetings, report writing, emails, and all of the daily admin that cried out for my attention. After some tough feedback from one of my teams, and great advice from my manager, I scheduled time every day just for spending time with my team. I sat with people to see what they were working on, walked the floor and asked people how they were doing; I'd see if I could "catch people doing things right!" and then appreciate them. People found it a little strange at first but soon adjusted, and it was a practice that helped me to build a culture where appreciation and connection was more normal. I felt happier at work and I think other people did too.

...A Therapist or Coach

Managers can be coaches, so this could be for you too. You may already know that appreciating people can be a wonderful intervention to help grow a sense of self-worth, and understanding how we positively impact the world around us. You could also use this book to teach clients how to appreciate themselves, their loved ones, their colleagues, and anyone else! Whether you use it in your sessions, lend them a copy, or suggest buying a copy so they can practice at home and in work, this could be a valuable resource for you and the people you help. Get creative! I'm sure there are are lots of other uses you can put this to. Please let me know how you get on, I love to hear stories and others may benefit by your wisdom.

...A Trainer or Facilitator

This is my main role these days. As I have said, what I find when asking groups to appreciate each other is that people sometimes struggle with it, however, it can also be deeply valuable. Starting a day or session with everyone appreciating something in themselves, their lives, or each other can set people in a positive frame for learning. Closing a session or day asking people to appreciate the time together and perhaps one other person can create a lovely, warm ending. Teaching appreciation to managers, staff, or basically any human being can embed a vital skill while creating a positive atmosphere for learning and maybe even making the world a better place! Try it and let me know how you get on.

The Advanced Class,

other ways to practice,

and some of the research about appreciative approaches

The Advanced Class:

This isn't huge but it does take bringing your attention to... The first step could be to grow your practice from using the single words provided here to being more free-form in your appreciation-giving. I know, wild right?! But seriously, you can still use the start of the sentence you have perhaps got used to now:

What I appreciate about you is...

From there let your intuition guide you a bit. Be really present with the person you are appreciating, see them as clearly as you can in that moment and speak honestly, openly, from the heart. It might feel risky but I think life is more vivid with such moments of valuable vulnerability.

The 30 Day Challenge

I have talked about appreciation as a practice and if you want to be both consistent and skilful at it I believe that is what it needs to be: something you do regularly and bring attention to refining. When we learn new skills we build new connections between the neurons (cells) in our brains. At first these connections are weak and if they are not cultivated they will shrink and disappear. The more you repeat a behaviour, the bigger and stronger the connections become until that skill you have been learning becomes a habit - it's second nature, requiring little thought. That is what practice is for: taking a skill and cultivating it through care and repetition into a positive habit. Apparently, to establish a new connection to the point it won't fade takes about 30 days of consistent daily practice. So… if you want to build appreciation into your life in a lasting way then the place to start is to give at least one mindful appreciation every day for 30 days. That's the 30 day challenge.

The anecdotal evidence around longer term behavioural change is that it seems to take 90 days consistent practice of a new way of being to give it the best chance of really sticking long term. So if you want to be a full-on appreciation ninja then 90 days is the way to go. 90 days can feel like a lot though so don't overwhelm yourself, why not start with 30 days and see how it goes? Then maybe you can do another 30 days. One more set and you have your 90, but you have done it in manageable chunks. There's the gauntlet thrown down, are you up for the 30 day challenge?

Blanket Appreciation

For any of you out there who are already master appreciators, if you've practiced a bunch and want another step, or even if you just want a slightly different way to welcome appreciation into your life, here's another practice: Blanket Appreciation. In this you bring your attention to just appreciating the bejeesus out of everything you come across - not just people, things too. In your mind, as you move through your life, this is an opportunity to more fully notice the world around you. Each person or thing you notice, you take a moment to appreciate.

Just as with regular appreciation, the more specific you can be about what quality of a person or thing you are appreciating the better: a building being strong and enduring, a yellow line down the side of the road keeping people safe, a flower adding a splash of colour and delicacy to the world. Whatever it is, you notice and appreciate its unique gifts.

In some ways, noticing and appreciating things that you otherwise wouldn't notice, those things that fade into the background, can be both the best challenge and the richest opportunity. It's an opportunity to transform your world into one filled with wonderful things and unique gifts. Who wouldn't want to live in a world so blessed? And all the while you are doing that you are refining your skills of appreciation, perfecting your practice, honing your habit...

6 minutes to relationship richness

My wife and I have a 3 year old son which as you may know means we have been sleep deprived for well over 3 years and are kept very busy even when not 'working.' We wanted to find a way to connect as a couple more often and not let our relationship slide into disrepair. So, I borrowed one of the Frameworks4Change habits and we started our 6 minutes a day: 3 minutes each where one speaks and the other just listens (no interrupting, not even questions), then offer one appreciation to each other. It's brief enough that even on crazy days we can manage it, and it helps us share stories and stay connected. I think this could work for any relationship: family, work, friendship – try it and see how it works for you :-)

Research...

in case you're interested...

There are a number of studies which seem to show that appreciation is beneficial, even necessary to achieving best results. Here are a few that I'm aware of in case they help you embrace the work even more:

The Magic Ratio: Dr. John Gottman in studying relationships, and researchers Emily Heaphy and Marcial Losada in studying organisations have found that there seems to be some kind of optimal ratio of appreciation and positive comments to criticism and negative comments. While some of the specifics of these numbers have been questioned since the original research (particularly for Losada and Heaphy) it seems solid that some kind of ratio which averages out between 5:1 and 6:1 appreciation to criticism creates the best emotional environment for people and relationships to thrive. So while some constructive feedback is needed to keep people on track, how many places do you think have a normal culture of 5 or 6 appreciations for every criticism? In my experience, most places need more appreciation in their conversations!

Pygmalion Studies: There have been numerous repeats of a study where you take a class of children, randomly assign them ranks in the class (top tier, middle tier, bottom tier) for performance and then introduce a teacher and give them those rankings as if they were how the children have genuinely been performing... And guess what? Six months later, the children are performing in line with their initially randomly assigned level of performance! So not only is our performance affected by what we believe, it is affected by what other people believe of us, even when that is not based on anything but a random allocation! It's not full-proof but people will develop in the direction of our judgements about them. If we work to appreciate each other, maybe we can all learn and grow.

Self-Monitoring: In sports and athletics a lot of research has been done into the effect on performance of the use of positive images. Particularly in sports coaching, studies have been done to see the difference between focusing on fixing the faults (negative self-monitoring) from previous performance, or re-enforcing the positive (positive self-monitoring). This was done by watching back (on video) and analysing previous performance. The test groups using positive self-monitoring have consistently performed better in these trials and have at times shown improvements of up to 100%. Through appreciation of each other we can help to embed positive self-monitoring as a habit which is likely to make us more effective as well as, very likely, happier![1]

There are other bodies of research out there which support the value of appreciation, but hopefully this helps to validate the need for this work for those of you who find that kind of thing important in your learning.

---

1   References for the first example can be found prolifically online, these second two I have drawn from a paper by Dr. David Cooperider, founder of Appreciative Inquiry. See his paper "Positive Image, Positive Action: The Affirmative Basis of Organising."

"What I appreciate about you is your..."

Author Profile

Francis trained originally as an actor, then ran away from the circus to find his home.

These days he is primarily a facilitator and writer. His work seems to have organised itself into five broad themes: Embodiment, Compassion, Conscious Leadership, Positive Psychology, and Sustainability.

If you'd like to know more about his work, access free resources, do an online course or read Francis' blog go to:

www.fudoshin.org.uk

To find out more about the work which inspired this book focusing on growing cultures and legacies of compassion, particularly in health and social care, see:

www.frameworks4change.co.uk

The Little Book of Appreciation

"What I appreciate about you is your..."

"What I appreciate about you is your..."

The Little Book of Appreciation
"What I appreciate about you is your..."